HOPE
FOR US
KNOWING GOD THROUGH THE NICENE CREED

Natasha Sistrunk Robinson

Hope for Us

Copyright © 2017 by Natasha Sistrunk Robinson

All rights reserved. No part of this book may be reproduced, stored in a retrieval system, or transmitted in any from or by any means without written permission from Natasha Sistrunk Robinson. Requests for information, speaking and consulting requests maybe sent through the official process at her official website: www.natashaSrobinson.com

Published in the United States by Credo House Publishers,
a division of Credo Communications, LLC, Grand Rapids, Michigan
credohousepublishers.com

Natasha Sistrunk Robinson is the Visionary Founder of Leadership LINKS, Inc. The organization offers leadership education that facilitates impactful living character and spiritual development. 10% of all proceeds from this resource will support the mission of Leadership LINKS. Find out more: www.leadershiplinksus.org

ISBN: 978-1-625860-85-9

Scripture taken from the Holy Bible, New International Version™ NIV. Copyright © 1973, 1978, 1984, 2011 by Biblica. Used by permission of Zondervan. All rights reserved worldwide.

Scholarly Review - This resource has been reviewed by:

Donald M. Fairbairn, Jr. Ph.D.
Academic Dean, Charlotte Campus
Robert E. Cooley Professor of Early Christianity
Gordon-Conwell Theological Seminary

Esau McCaulley, Ph.D.
Assistant Professor of New Testament and Early Christianity
Northeastern Seminary

Christopher Alan Hall, Ph.D.
President, Renovaré

Cover Design: Nicolas Mulder
Interior Design: Nicolas Mulder

Printed in the United States of America

CONTENTS

Nicene Creed i

Introduction iii

History of the Nicene Creed v

Lesson One   God Is One 1

Lesson Two   Jesus Is God 5

Lesson Three   Jesus Is the Hope of Our Salvation 13

Lesson Four   The Holy Spirit is God 27

Lesson Five   Sustaining Work of the Holy Spirit 33

Lesson Six   The Church as a People of God 43

List of Definitions 61

Appendixes 65

Endnotes 69

About the Author 73

About "Mentor for Life" 75

About Leadership LINKS, Inc. 76

INTRODUCTION

I love leading and training people to mentor and multiply for God's kingdom purposes. This mentorship, is also known as intentional discipleship, and it is about teaching people how to become a follower of Jesus Christ.

The mentoring framework that I have outlined includes:

1. Knowing and Loving God,
2. Affirming our Identity in Christ Jesus, and
3. Loving our Neighbors.

If we are to understand our life's purpose, we must first begin with God. The theologian A. W. Tozer wrote, "What comes to our minds when we think about God is the most important thing about us."[3] If we have a distorted view of God, then we will have an incorrect view of ourselves and also, an incorrect view of others.

Who is God? What is the nature of God? Who are we?

God desires that we know him. It is not until we come to understand who God is, that we can confirm who we are as the people of God, his church. Knowing and loving God, and affirming our identity in Christ are both necessary if we are to love our neighbors well. It is with this understanding—this desire to gain "Knowledge" or "Know God"—that we humbly approach our study of the Nicene Creed.

Through this study, we will first answer the question: What does the Nicene Creed say about God and about the church? Then we will answer the question: What does the Nicene Creed mean? Finally, we will explore together the significance of these truths for our own lives.

HOW TO USE THIS STUDY

This study is organized into lessons, and not weeks. The reason for this organization is to ensure that you are working through the material at your own pace, and that you are actually growing in knowledge without unnecessary time constraints. If you are going through this study with a small group, then I recommend that the group determines how much material you will cover within a certain amount of time.

People will be approaching this study from different places on their spiritual journey, so I have taken the liberty to include foot or endnotes that provide clarifying information, a dictionary of terms which can be found in the back of the study, and I have also included a visual aid along with additional scriptures to continue your future study on the topic of the Holy Trinity.

The terms found in the dictionary will be shown with a dashed underline.

To get the most out of the study, it is important that you read through all of the scriptures and answer the questions that are provided. The questions and reflections are provided to reinforce your learning.

In Psalm 119:11 we find the words, "I have hidden your word in my heart that I might not sin against you." Each lesson includes a scripture for memorization. Knowing and memorizing scripture informs us of God's truth. Scripture memorization also helps us understand and grow closer to God. Finally, memorizing scripture guards our heart against sin, anything we do that falls short of God's holy standard.

HISTORY OF THE NICENE CREED[4]

Fundamental to the Christian faith is the ability to answer the question:

Who is Jesus?

This is the most important question for today's Christian, and it was the most important question for the ancient Christian community. Early Christian leaders prayerfully talked about this question at length at what is known as *ecumenical councils*.

The Council of Nicaea and the Council of Constantinople are the first two of seven ecumenical councils. The purpose of the councils was to determine, gain clarity, and consensus concerning the basic fundamentals of the Christian faith.

Can you imagine the challenge of trying to accurately articulate the being or nature of God, trying to make a distinction between the Father and the Son while still affirming belief in only one God, and trying to properly communicate the relationship between the Father, the Son, and the Holy Spirit, when these ideas had not been articulated with any level of authority or assurance previously?

FIRST ECUMENICAL COUNCIL (NICAEA I) & THE CREED OF NICAEA (N)

The first Ecumenical[5] Council, the Council of Nicaea[6] (Nicaea I), convened on May 20, 325 for two months. From this council, the church got the Creed of Nicaea (which scholars and theologians refer to as "N").

The Creed of Nicaea took care to emphasize the word *homoousios*, a word that expressed that the Father and Son shared the same essence or being. Their debate centered on a fundamental question: *Is Jesus God?*

At one point, a popular preacher named Arius (256-336) proposed the idea that Jesus was the most exalted creature that God the Father had ever created. He concluded that it is not possible for a human being to be god. He was condemned as a heretic for teaching that Jesus, the Son, was a creature—a *created being*—with a beginning at some point in the will of God, and that Jesus was not God. This false teaching became known as the Arian Heresy and it: a.) denied the deity of Christ, b.) taught that only God the Father is eternal, while his Son (Jesus) was the first and highest created being, and c.) that the Son is not one in essence with the Father.

At this time, a Christian theologian named Athanasius argued that only God can save human beings from sin. Human beings cannot save themselves from sin, only God can do that. Therefore, if Jesus is not God, then Jesus cannot save us.

After much debate, the council resolved that Jesus was and is God.

While the question of the Son and his deity was affirmed, the questions concerning the nature of the Holy Spirit continued to linger. The original creed adopted at the Council of Nicaea in 325 ended before the words, "We believe in the Holy Spirit." The Creed of Nicaea is like a rough draft of what was finalized and expanded in 381 to become what we refer to as the "Nicene Creed."

SECOND ECUMENICAL COUNCIL (CONSTANTINOPLE I) AND THE NICENE CREED (C)

Questions concerning the deity of the Holy Spirit were more thoroughly addressed at the Council of Constantinople which began on January 10, 381. At this council, the faith of Nicaea was affirmed, and the full deity of the Holy Spirit was declared.

From this council and the debates that occurred, we receive the Nicene Creed (more accurately referred to by scholars as the Niceno or Nicene-Constantinopolitan Creed). "It is the profession of the Christian Faith common to the Catholic Church,[7] and to most of the Protestant denominations. As a result of this creed, the position of the church in the East was firmly established: The Father is God; Jesus, the Son, is God; the Holy Spirit is God; and God is one.

Affirming the deity of the Holy Spirit was a definitive feature of this creed. "The Spirit is acknowledged in biblical terms as 'the Lord' (2 Cor. 3:17) and 'the life-giver' (2 Cor. 3:6) and as jointly worshipped with the Father and the Son."[8] Regarding the nature of God, therefore, the church's conclusion is "there are three eternal *hypostaseis* [persons], all on the same level of divine being, distinct yet indivisible…Not only were the Son and the Spirit coequal with the Father; all three were together declared to be one God."[9]

Not only did this creed state the nature of God, it also affirmed the nature of the church being "one, holy, catholic, and apostolic." During the Protestant Reformation, these became known as the four "Nicene notes" of the church, as characteristic and defining markers.

What is the significance of the Nicene Creed?

After the Holy Bible, the Nicene Creed is the only statement in Christian history that is accepted by all groups of the Christian church. Every group of Christians—that does not hold a principled objection to the concept of creeds—affirms the Nicene Creed.

THE NICENE CREED

I believe in one God, the Father Almighty, Maker of heaven and earth, and of all things visible and invisible.

I believe in one Lord Jesus Christ, the only-begotten Son of God, born of the Father before all ages. God from God, Light from Light, true God from true God; begotten, not made, consubstantial[1] with the Father, through him all things were made. For us men and for our salvation, he came down from heaven, and by the Holy Spirit was incarnate of the Virgin Mary, and became man. **For our sake, he was crucified under Pontius Pilate; He suffered** *death and was buried; and rose again on the third day in accordance with the Scriptures. He ascended into heaven, and is seated at the right hand of the Father. He will come again in glory to judge the living and the dead, and his kingdom will have no end.*

I believe in the Holy Spirit, the Lord, the Giver of Life; who proceeds from the Father and the Son;[1] who with **the Father and the Son is adored and glorified, who has spoken through the** *prophets. I believe in one, holy, catholic and apostolic Church. I confess one baptism for the forgiveness of sins, and I look forward to the resurrection of the dead and the life of the world to come. Amen.*[2]

---

1   *Consubstantial* means "of the same substance."

Study Outline:

For the purposes of this study, the Nicene Creed is outlined into three articles focusing on the themes of each Lesson.

Article I focuses on teachings concerning God, the Father (Lesson One).

I believe in one God, the Father Almighty, Maker of heaven and earth, and of all things visible and invisible.

Article II focuses on the divinity of God, the Son, and is divided into two parts. Part I is taught in Lesson Two and it reveals that Jesus, the Son, is God. Part II is taught in Lesson Three and it references the salvation that Jesus offers.

Part I: *I believe in one Lord Jesus Christ, the only-begotten Son of God, born of the Father before all ages. God from God, Light from Light, true God from true God; begotten, not made, consubstantial with the Father, through him all things were made. For us men and for our salvation, he came down from heaven, and by the Holy Spirit was incarnate of the Virgin Mary, and became man.*

Part II: *For our sake, he was crucified under Pontius Pilate; He suffered death and was buried; and rose again on the third day in accordance with the Scriptures. He ascended into heaven, and is seated at the right hand of the Father. He will come again in glory to judge the living and the dead, and his kingdom will have no end.*

Article III focuses on the Divinity and work of the Holy Spirit, and the nature of the Church. Lesson Four references the Divinity of the Holy Spirit. Lesson Five focuses on the sustaining work of the Holy Spirit. Lesson Six speaks to the nature of the church as a people of God.

I believe in the Holy Spirit, the Lord, the Giver of Life; who proceeds from the Father and the Son; who with the **Father and the Son is adored and glorified, who has spoken through the** *prophets. I believe in one, holy, catholic and apostolic Church. I confess one baptism for the forgiveness of sins, and I look forward to the resurrection of the dead and the life of the world to come. Amen.*

LESSON ONE:
GOD IS ONE

Scripture Memorization: *Hear, O Israel: The Lord our God, the Lord is one.* Deuteronomy 6:4

Article I: I believe in one God, the Father Almighty, Maker of heaven and earth, and of all things visible and invisible.

Take-away: Christianity is a monotheistic faith, meaning that Christians serve only one God. God the Father, God the Son, and God the Holy Spirit are one, not three gods.

I believe in **one God**, the Father Almighty.

Truth: God is one.

Christianity is a relational faith. What does this statement communicate about the Christian's understanding of his or her relationship to God?

Sometimes it is difficult to embrace God as our spiritual Father because our relationships with our earthly fathers are so broken. How has your relationship been with your earthly father over the years?

Our God is a good Father. What do good fathers do?

> I believe in one God, the Father Almighty, **Maker of** heaven and earth, and of all things visible and invisible.

Truth: God is the creator of **all** things.

Read the creation account of Genesis Chapters 1 and 2 in your Bible.

Write a paragraph summary of what you see taking place in these scriptures:

Make a list of the things God created as mentioned in Genesis Chapters 1 and 2:

How do we see God the Father and God the Holy Spirit at work in these passages? In the next lesson, you will notice that God the Son is also at work in creation.

Read Romans Chapter 8, verses 38-39, to discover the power of God's love throughout creation.

> *^{38} For I am convinced that neither death nor life, neither angels nor demons, neither the present nor the future, nor any powers, ^{39} neither height nor depth, nor anything else in all creation, will be able to separate us from the love of God that is in Christ Jesus our Lord.*

What confidence, if any, do these passages give you about your personal relationship with God?

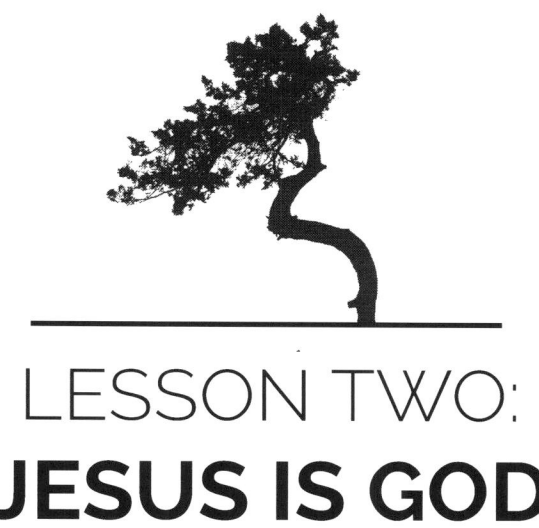

LESSON TWO:
JESUS IS GOD

Scripture Memorization: *Jesus answered, "I am the way and the truth and the life. No one comes to the Father except through me. If you really knew me, you would know my Father as well. From now on, you do know him and have seen him."* John 14:6-7

Article II: I believe in one Lord Jesus Christ, the only-begotten Son of God, born of the Father before all ages. God from God, Light from Light, true God from true God; begotten, not made, consubstantial with the Father, through him all things were made.

Article II, about the Son, is divided into two parts—the first part focuses on who Jesus is eternally, and the second focuses on what he did through the incarnation for our salvation.

Take-away: The only way to understand and enter into right relationship with the Father, God, is through his Son, Jesus.

Truth: The Son is God.

Read the gospel of John Chapter 1, verses 1-4 to discover Jesus' hand in creation.

> *¹ In the beginning was the Word* [reference to Jesus who has always existed as the Son of God], *and the Word was with God, and the Word was God. ² He was with God in the beginning. ³ Through him all things were made; without him nothing was made that has been made. ⁴ In him was life, and that life was the light of men.*

According to these scriptures, what role did Jesus play in creation?

Do these passages confirm that Jesus is God? If so, how do they confirm it?

> I believe in one **Lord Jesus Christ, the** only-begotten **Son of God**, born of the Father before **all ages [or before all worlds]**. God from God, Light from Light, true God from true God; begotten, not made, consubstantial[2] with the Father, through him all things were made.

Truth: Jesus is one with the Father, God; therefore, Jesus is God.

Read John 14:8-11:

> *⁸ Philip said, "Lord, show us the Father and that will be enough for us." ⁹ Jesus answered: Don't you know me, Philip, even after I have been among you such a long time? Anyone who has seen me has seen the Father. How can you say, 'Show us the Father'? ¹⁰ Don't you believe that I am **in** the Father, and that the Father is **in me?** The words I say to you are not just my own. Rather, it is the Father, living **in** me, who is doing his work. ¹¹ Believe me when I say that I am **in** the Father and the Father is in me; or at least believe on the evidence of the miracles themselves.*

What does Jesus say about his relationship with God the Father in this passage?

---

[2] Consubstantial means "of the same substance."

Write down John 14:11.

Read Jesus' prayer in John 17:20-23:

*²⁰ My prayer is not for them [his disciples] alone. I pray also for those who will believe in me through their message. ²¹ that all of them may be **one**, Father, just as you are **in** me and I am **in** you. May they also be in us so that the world may believe that you have sent me. ²² I have given them the glory that you have me, that they may be **one** as we are **one**. ²³ I in them and you **in** me. May they be brought to complete unity to let the world know that you sent me and have loved them even as you have loved me.*

What does Jesus reveal about his relationship with God, the Father, in these passages?

Knowledge Checkpoint: Go back and read John 14:8-11 and John 17:20-23 again. Circle every time you see the word "believe."

What does Jesus want us to believe?

Read John 10: 24-33:

²⁴ The Jews gathered around him, saying, "How long will you keep us in suspense?" If you are the Christ, tell us plainly. ²⁵ Jesus answered, "I did tell you, but you do not believe. The miracles I do in my Father's name speak for me, ²⁶ but you do not believe because you are not my sheep [a metaphor for the people who belong to Jesus, those who have salvation, and those who are in a right relationship with God]. ²⁷ My sheep listen to my voice; I know *them, and they follow me. ²⁸ I give them <u>eternal</u> life, and they shall never <u>perish</u>; no one can snatch them out of my hand. ²⁹ My Father, who has given them to me, is greater than all; no one can snatch them out of my Father's hand. ³⁰ I and the Father are one." ³¹ Again the Jews picked up stones to stone him, ³² but Jesus said to them, "I have shown you many great miracles from the Father. For which of these do you stone me?" ³³ "We are not stoning you for any of these," replied the Jews, "but for <u>blasphemy</u>, because you, a mere man, claim to be God."*

According to Jesus, what do the miracles that he performed prove?

What did Jesus say about the people who are described as his sheep?

1. Sheep l_____ to the voice of God.

2. Sheep are k_____ by God.

3. Sheep f_____ God.

4. Sheep receive e_____ l_____ from God.

5. Sheep will never p_____.

6. No one will ever s_____ the sheep out of God's h_____.

What hope do these words provide about your relationship with Jesus if you believe?

LESSON TWO: JESUS IS GOD

What does Jesus say about his relationship with the Father, God, in this passage?

Write down John 10:30.

According to John 10:30-33, what was the reason people were trying to kill Jesus?

Truth: Jesus is the _only-begotten_ Son of God.

Read John 10:34-39:

> [34] Jesus answered them, "Is it not written in your Law, 'I have said you are gods[10]? [35] If he called them 'gods,' to whom the word of God came—and the Scripture cannot be broken—[36] what about the one [speaking of himself] whom the Father set apart as his very own and sent into the world? Why then do you accuse me of _blasphemy_ because I said, 'I am God's Son'? [37] Do not believe me unless I do what my Father does. [38] But if I do it, even though you do not believe me, believe the miracles, that you may know and understand that the Father is **in** me, and I **in** the Father. [39] Again they tried to seize him, but he escaped their grasp.

Note: Throughout these passages, Jesus refers to himself as the Son in relationship with God the Father. The understanding of this language is that God the Father has always been a father because he has always had a Son in Jesus, who was always in existence. (The Son became incarnate through the miraculous birth of Jesus. That is when Jesus' divine nature was joined to his human nature at a specific point in time.) Therefore, Father is not just a *metaphor* to describe God. In this case, however imperfectly, the word "Father" is used as an *archetype*, a very typical example of a certain person or thing. We must acknowledge from these scriptures that our earthly relationships—even our familial ones—are meant to reflect the spiritual relationship of God. We serve a relational God, who has always been in relationship with himself, and he longs to be in relationship with us.

Truth: Jesus has both a human and divine nature. The Word or divine nature of Jesus, the Son of God, has always existed. The human nature of Jesus did not always exist. The miracle of the incarnation reveals the moment in time when the Son's divine nature was joined to his human nature.

Read 1 Timothy 1:8-10.

> *⁸ "So do not be ashamed to testify about our Lord, or ashamed of me [the writer is Paul] his prisoner. But join with me in suffering for the gospel, by the power of God, ⁹ who has saved us and called us to a holy life—not because of anything we have done but because of his own purpose and grace. This grace was given us in Christ Jesus before the beginning of time, ¹⁰ but it has now been revealed through the appearing of our Savior, Christ Jesus, who has destroyed death and has brought life and immortality to light through the gospel.*

What do we learn about Christ in these passages?

Read John 1:1-4.

> *¹ In the beginning was the Word [named for Jesus], and the Word was with God, and the Word was God. ² He was with God in the beginning. ³ Through him all things were made; without him nothing was made that has been made. ⁴ In him was life, and that life was the light of men.*

What is the relationship between Jesus and the Word?

When was Jesus with God, the Father? According to this passage, has he always been with the Father?

According to this passage, what role did Jesus play in creation?

Read Hebrews 1:1-3 in your Bible.

Hebrews 1:3a:

> *The Son is the radiance of God's glory and the exact representation of his being, sustaining all things by his powerful word…*

What do we learn about Jesus in these verses?

Read Colossians 1:15-17:

> *15 He is the image of the invisible God, the firstborn over all creation 16 For by him all things were created: things in heaven and on earth, visible and invisible, whether thrones or powers or rulers or authorities; all things were created by him and for him. 17 He is before all things, and in him all things hold together.*

What do these passages reveal about Christ's continuous work throughout creation? Can anyone other than God do this?

LESSON THREE:
JESUS IS THE HOPE OF OUR SALVATION

Scripture Memorization: *That if you confess with your mouth, "Jesus is Lord," and believe in your heart that God raised him from the dead, you will be saved. For it is with your heart that you believe and are justified, and it is with your mouth that you confess and are saved.* Romans 10:9-10

> **Article II:** For us men and for our salvation, he came down from heaven, and by the Holy Spirit was incarnate of the Virgin Mary, and became man. For our sake, he was crucified under Pontius Pilate; He suffered death and was buried; and rose again on the third day in accordance with the Scriptures. He ascended into heaven, and is seated at the right hand of the Father. He will come again in glory to judge the living and the dead, and his kingdom will have no end.

Article II, about the Son, is divided into two parts—the first part focuses on who Jesus is <u>eternally</u>, and the second focuses on what he did through the <u>incarnation</u> for our <u>salvation</u>.

Take-away: Jesus alone offers the hope of our <u>salvation</u>.

> For us men and **for our <u>salvation</u>, he came down from heaven,** and **by the Holy Spirit was <u>incarnate</u> of the Virgin Mary, and became man.**
>
> **for our <u>salvation</u>, he came down from heaven:**

Truth: "For Christ died for sins once for all, the righteous for the unrighteous, to bring you to God. He was put to death in the body but made alive by the Spirit (1 Peter 3:18)."

HOPE FOR US

Read John 3:16-17:

> ¹⁶ *For God so loved the world that he gave his one and only Son, that whoever believes in him shall not perish but have eternal life.* ¹⁷ *For God did not send his Son into the world to condemn the world, but to save the world through him.*

Read Romans 8:1-2:

> *1 Therefore, there is now no condemnation for those who are in Christ Jesus, 2 because through Christ Jesus the law of the Spirit of life set me free from the law of sin and death.*

Read John 6:38-40:

> ³⁸ *For I have come down from heaven not to do my will but to do the will of him who sent me.* ³⁹ *And this is the will of him who sent me, that I shall lose none of all that he has given me, but raise them up at the last day.* ⁴⁰ *For my Father's will is that everyone who looks to the Son and believes in him shall have eternal life, and I will raise him up at the last day."*

What do these passages reveal about Jesus' life's mission and purpose?

What are Jesus' promises for all those who believe in him?

What hope does this truth offer us?

> by the Holy Spirit was incarnate of the Virgin Mary, and became man:

Truth: The Son of God was always divine, but he was not always human. Because of the incarnation, Jesus is fully divine and is fully human through birth.

The are several prophecies in the Old Testament regarding the birth of Jesus. Write down one of them from Isaiah 7:14:

Read Matthew 1:18-2:23. Summarize what you have learned about Jesus' birth in these passages:

According to Matthew 1:21, why was the name "Jesus" given to the incarnate Son?

According to Matthew 1:23, why would Jesus also be called "Immanuel"? What does that mean?

Read Luke 1:26-35. Summarize what you have learned about Jesus' birth in these passages:

> **For our sake, he [Jesus] was crucified** under Pontius Pilate; **He suffered death and was buried; and rose again on the third day in accordance with the Scriptures.**
>
> **For our sake, he [Jesus] was crucified under Pontius Pilate:**

Read about Jesus' trial under the Roman Governor, Pontius Pilate in Matthew 27:11-26, Mark 15:1-15, Luke 22:66-23:25, and John 18:28-19:16.

Take Notes:

LESSON THREE: JESUS IS THE HOPE OF OUR SALVATION

According to Mark 15:9-10, why did the chief priests hand Jesus over to Pilate?

What was the charge against Jesus? Reference Mark 15:26; Luke 22:70-23:23, 38; and John 19:7, 12-15, 19-22. Were any of the charges true?

Quick Reference: Read John 10:24-39 to see an example of the tension that was building between the truth that Jesus offered, and what the Jews had come to believe as true. What is happening in this scripture?

What was Jesus' initial response to the charges?

Write down Jesus' response in John 18:36:

What is the significance of this statement?

What was the judicial verdict?

According to Jesus' response in John 18:37, what was his life's purpose?

He suffered death and was buried:

Read about Jesus' suffering, death by crucifixion, and burial in Matthew 27:27-61, Mark 15:16-47, Luke 23:26-56, and John 19:16-42.

Take Notes:

What was Jesus' response to his suffering in Matthew 27:46?

LESSON THREE: JESUS IS THE HOPE OF OUR SALVATION

Do you ever feel forsaken by God? In those moments, what are some of your thoughts?

What hope does Jesus offer us even when we feel forsaken?

At his death, what was the conclusion drawn about Jesus? Reference Matthew 27:54, Mark 15:39.

rose again on the third day:

Read about Jesus' **resurrection** in Matthew 27:62-28:15, Mark 16:1-8, Luke 24:1-11, John 20:1-9

Note: Luke 24:12-49, John 20:10-21:25, and Acts 10:39-41 record the occasions where Jesus revealed himself to his follows after his resurrection.

Take Notes:

According to these scriptures, what actually happened to Jesus' body after his death?

According to these scriptures, what was reported about Jesus' body after his death?

> He [Jesus] ascended into heaven, and is seated at the right hand of the Father. **He will come again** in glory to judge the living and the dead, and his kingdom will have no end.

The Ascent:
What does the Bible say about Jesus' ascent? Write down Ephesians 4:9-10:

Read Luke 24:50-52 and Acts 1:1-11. What promise do we have concerning Jesus in these passages?

Read 1 Peter 3:18-22:

> ¹⁸ *For Christ died for sins once for all, the righteous for the unrighteous, to bring you to God. He was put to death in the body but made alive by the Spirit,* ¹⁹ *through whom also he went and preached to the spirits in prison* ²⁰ *who disobeyed long ago when God waited patiently in the days of Noah while the ark was being built. In it only a few people, eight in all, were saved through water,* ²¹ *and this water symbolizes baptism that now saves you also—not the removal of dirt from the body but the pledge of a good conscience toward God. It saves you by the resurrection of Jesus Christ,* ²² *who has gone into heaven and is at God's right hand—with the angels, authorities and powers in submission to him.*

LESSON THREE: JESUS IS THE HOPE OF OUR SALVATION

According to verse 18, why did Jesus die?

According to these verses, where do you see the Holy Spirit at work?

According to the scriptures, Jesus is presently with the Father doing the following work:

a.) Jesus is now preparing a place for us. Read Jesus' promise in John 14:1-4:

> *¹ "Do not let your hearts be troubled. Trust in God; trust also in me. ² In my Father's house are many rooms; if it were not so, I would have told you. <u>I am going there to prepare a place for you. ³ And if I go and prepare a place for you, I will come back and take you to be with me that you also may be where I am.</u> ⁴ You know the way to the place where I am going."*

He continued to teach and comfort his <u>disciples</u> with the promises found in John 14:28-29:

> *²⁸ <u>"You heard me say, 'I am going away and I am coming back to you.'</u> If you loved me, you would be glad that I am going to the Father, for the Father is greater than I. ²⁹ I have told you now before it happens, so that when it does happen you will believe."*

Truth: Jesus is right now preparing this place for our dwelling. As his own death drew near, he used a <u>metaphor</u> of a house to describe the new <u>eternal</u> world he is creating.

b.) Jesus is now interceding on our behalf. Read Romans 8:31-39.

When writing a letter to the Christians in Rome, Paul asks important questions regarding our <u>eternal</u> life and relationship with God. He also offers hope and assurance for those of us who believe in Jesus. Read Romans 8:31-39:

> *³¹ What, then, shall we say in response to this? If God is for us, who can be against us? ³² He who did not spare his own Son, but gave him up for us all—how will he not also, along with him, graciously give us all things? ³³ Who will bring any charge against those whom God has chosen?* ***It is God who justifies.*** *³⁴ Who is he that condemns? Christ Jesus, who died—more than that, who was raised to life—is at <u>the right hand of God</u> and is also interceding for us. ³⁵ Who shall separate*

> us from the love of Christ? Shall trouble or hardship or persecution or famine or nakedness or danger or sword? ³⁶ As it is written:
>> "For your sake we face death all day long;
>> We are considered as sheep to be slaughtered (Psalm 44:22)."
>
> ³⁷ No, in all these things we are more than conquerors through him who loved us. ³⁸ For I am convinced that neither death nor life, neither angels nor demons, neither the present nor the future, nor any powers, ³⁹ neither height nor depth, nor anything else in all creation, will be able to separate us from the love of God that is in Christ Jesus our Lord.

Can anything at all separate us from the love of God that is in Christ Jesus?

Read Hebrews 7:23-25:

> ²³ Now there have been many of those priests, since death prevented them from continuing in office; ²⁴ but <u>because Jesus lives forever</u>, he has a permanent priesthood. ²⁵ **Therefore he is able to save completely** those who come to God through him, because <u>he always lives to intercede for them.</u>

Truth: Jesus is the righteous judge. There will be judgement of our works of righteous for our <u>eternal</u> reward. The guilty, who reject God, will be judged to receive their <u>eternal</u> punishment.

Read Jesus' words in Revelation 22:12:

> "Behold, I am coming soon! My reward is with me, and I will give to everyone according to what he has done.

Read 1 Corinthians 3:10-15 in your Bible. Take notes:

LESSON THREE: JESUS IS THE HOPE OF OUR SALVATION

How do these scriptures encourage us to build and work in God's kingdom? What or who is our foundation?

Read John 5:22-30 in your Bible. Take notes:

What promises do we receive from these scriptures?

Read Acts 17:30-31:

> *30 In the past God overlooked such ignorance, but now he commands all people everywhere to repent. 31 For he has set a day when he will judge the world with justice by the man he has appointed. He has given proof of this to all men by raising him from the dead."*

Read Acts 10:42-43:

> *42 He commanded us to preach to the people and to testify that he is the one whom God appointed as judge of the living and the dead. 43 All the prophets testify about him that everyone who believes in him receives forgiveness of sins through his name."*

Read 2 Timothy 4:8:

> *Now there is in store for me [Paul is writing] the crown of righteousness which the Lord, the righteous Judge, will award to me on that day—and not only to me, but also to all who have longed for his appearing.*

According to these verses, what promises do we receive from Christ?

Read 2 Corinthians 5:9-10 in your Bible. What encouragement do you see in these verses? What should be our life's goal?

> and his [Jesus] **kingdom will have no end.**

In the Bible, the gospel of Matthew, Chapter 1 records a genealogy of Jesus. In it, we find that he is from the linage of King David. Jesus is the answer to the covenantal promise God made with David (see 2 Samuel 7:8-16):

Read Psalm 89:19-29 in your Bible. What is recorded about the covenant God made with David in verses 28-29?

Read 2 Samuel 7:16:

> *Your house and your kingdom will endure forever before me; your throne will be established forever.*

Read Isaiah 9:6-7 about the prophecy of Christ. Write down the importance of these verses:

Read Luke 1:32-33:

> *³² The Lord will give him the throne of his father David, ³³ and he will reign over the house of Jacob forever; his kingdom will never end."*

What hope do these scriptures offer for our life with Jesus?

How do we know that this new kingdom that Jesus has made possible will have no end?

LESSON FOUR:
THE HOLY SPIRIT IS GOD

Scripture Memorization: *But you will receive power when the Holy Spirit comes on you; and you will be my witnesses in Jerusalem, and in all Judea and Samaria, and to the ends of the earth.* Acts 1:8

Article III: I believe in the Holy Spirit, the Lord, the Giver of Life; who proceeds from the Father and the Son; who with the Father and the Son is adored and glorified, who has spoken through the prophets.

Take-away: The Holy Spirit gives us <u>eternal life</u> through Jesus Christ, our Lord.

What can we know about the Spirit?

Truth: The Holy Spirit brings us into relationship with God. He makes it possible for us to become sons and daughters, and to acknowledge God as our Father.

Read Galatians 4:3-7:

> *³ So also, when we were children, <u>we were in slavery</u> under the basic principles of the world. ⁴ But when the time had fully come, God sent his Son born of a woman, born under law, ⁵ to redeem those under law that we might receive the full rights of sons. ⁶ Because you are sons, God sent the Spirit of his Son into your hearts, the Spirit who calls out, "Abba [Aramaic language for Father], Father." ⁷ So you are <u>no longer a slave, but a son</u>; and since you are a son, <u>God has made you also an heir</u>.*

What does this scripture say about our former relationship with God in the world?

What does this scripture say about the relationship of those who are in right relationship with God?

What is the significance of this relationship change?

What role does the Holy Spirit play in this transformation?

Read Romans 8:5-17 in your Bible. Write a paragraph summary of your understanding of these scriptures:

Knowledge Checkpoint: What is the difference between the "mind of a sinful human" verses a "mind controlled by the Spirit" in this passage?

LESSON FOUR: THE HOLY SPIRIT IS GOD

	Mind and Body of a Sinful Human	**Mind and Body Controlled by the Spirit**
Verse 5		
Verse 6		
Verses 7-8		
Verse 10		
Verse 13		

According to Verse 9, how do you know if you have the Spirit of God?

According to Verse 11, what is the promise of those who have the Spirit of God?

Because the Spirit of God is living in us, what is our responsibility? According to Verses 12 and 13, how are we expected to respond to God?

The Holy Spirit sustains our relationship with the God, the Father. According to Verse 14-17, how is that relationship defined?

According to Verse 17, what is the condition that the writer outlines regarding our relationship with Christ? What does this mean? Hint: Read Romans 8:18-23.

> I believe in the Holy Spirit, **the Lord, the Giver of Life**; who proceeds from the Father and the Son; [11] who with the Father and the Son is adored and glorified; **who has spoken through the** prophets.

Take-away: The Holy Spirit was present in creation, does miraculous works that only God can do, and is united with the Father and Son; therefore, the Holy Spirit is God.

>   **A. Truth:** The Holy Spirit was present in creation, to give life to the world and life to all humankind.

What does Genesis 1:2 and Genesis 1:26 reveal about the presence of the Holy Spirit in creation?

What does Genesis 2:7 reveal about the work of the Holy Spirit in the creation of humankind?

B. What does Matthew 1:18 and 23 and Luke 1:26-35 reveal about the presence and work of the Holy Spirit in the incarnation of Jesus?

C. The Holy Spirit was present and active at Jesus' baptism, and with this passage we visibly see the full presence of the Triune God. What do you observe at the baptism of Jesus in Matthew 3:16-17?

LESSON FIVE:
SUSTAINING WORK OF THE HOLY SPIRIT

Scripture Memorization: *But the Counselor, the Holy Spirit, whom the Father will send in my name, will teach you all things and will remind you of everything I have said to you.* John 14:26

Article III: I believe in the Holy Spirit, the Lord, the Giver of Life; who proceeds from the Father and the Son; who with the Father and the Son is adored and glorified, who has spoken through the prophets.

Take-way: The Holy Spirit inspires the Word of God, increases our understanding, and guides us in all truth.

The Work of the Holy Spirit in the Old Testament and through the Word:

Truth: The breath of God, or the Holy Spirit, was present in the preaching, teaching, and writings of the prophets.

Write the scripture 2 Peter 1:20-21:

Write the scripture 2 Timothy 3:16-17:

According to these texts, who is the source of Scripture, and what is the purpose of Scripture?

Given this truth, do you think knowing and understanding the scripture is important? Why or why not?

Jesus gave the following promises and assurances concerning the Holy Spirit:

Read John 14:15-26 in your Bible.

According to John 14:15, 21, and 23-24, how does Jesus say that our love for him is communicated?

According to John 14:16-17, 26, what are four roles or responsibilities that the Holy Spirit plays in our lives?

1.

2.

3.

4.

According to John 14:16, how do we receive the Holy Spirit?

According to John 14:17 and 22-24, does everyone have the Holy Spirit? How do we know that we have the Holy Spirit?

Write down the promise that Jesus gave his disciples in John 14:18:

What is Jesus' promise to his disciples regarding the Holy Spirit in John 16:7?

Truth: The Holy Spirit is our Godly Counselor.

Jesus taught his disciples about the work of the Holy Spirit:

Read John 16:7-15 in your Bible.

According to John 16:8, what is the work of the Holy Spirit?

What is conviction? Write down the definition here:

Why will the identified convictions come?

Verse 9 – Conviction of Sin	
Verse 10 – Conviction of Righteousness	
Verse 11 – Conviction of Judgment	

LESSON FIVE: SUSTAINING WORK OF THE HOLY SPIRIT

Who is the prince of this world? According to verse 11, what is his fate?

What is condemnation? Write down the definition here:

What is the difference we see in the scripture between conviction and condemnation? According to Romans 8:1-2, what promise do we have as Christians?

According to John 16:13-15, what is the work of the Holy Spirit:

	The Holy Spirit is the Spirit of Truth.
Verse 13	1. Guide _____.
	2. Speak _____.
	3. Tell _____.

37

Verse 14	4. Bring _____ _____, and making _____ _____.
Verse 15	5. Take _____, and make _____.

God also grants us gifts through the Holy Spirit.

Truth: The Holy Spirit assures our salvation.

The most important gift we receive from the Holy Spirit is the assurance of our eternal salvation.

Read and then write down Ephesians 1:13-14:

Read and then write down 2 Corinthians 1:21-22:

Read 2 Corinthians 5:5 in your Bible. What do we learn about God, and our relationship with him in this verse?

Given these verses, what hope and promise do we have in Christ?

Truth: The Holy Spirit makes it possible for us to live as one, united people.

Read 1 Corinthians Chapter 12.

Take Notes:

According to 1 Corinthians 12:4-6, what do we learn about the Holy Spirit and the body of Christ (church or God's people)?

In verses 12-27, the writer is using the physical body as a metaphor to describe our relationship with other Christians in "the body of Christ." What are some key points that he wants us to understand about our relationship with God and with each other?

According to 1 Corinthians 12:1 and 7-11, what does the writer of these verses want us to understand about the spiritual gifts offered to us?

Throughout the Bible, we can notice several examples of spiritual gifts. These lists are not exhaustive, but they give us an understanding of the ways God prepares us to serve him, each other, and to advance his good work in the world. Write down the spiritual gifts you notice in the following passages:

1 Corinthians 12:28-30	Romans 12:6-8	Ephesians 4:11	1 Peter 4:10-11

According to Ephesians 4:12-16 and 1 Peter 4:10, what is the purpose of our spiritual gifts?

When we think about the spiritual gifts that the Holy Spirit offers, we realize that the gifts are not given to support our selfish ambitions or to build ourselves up with pride. The gifts are given for the benefit of God's people. God can help us check our motivations, and he can give us a godly perspective regarding the use of our spiritual gifts. What instruction and encouragement does he offer in 1 Corinthians 12:31, 13:13, and 14:12?

LESSON SIX:
THE CHURCH AS A PEOPLE OF GOD

Scripture Memorization: *Finally, all of you, live in harmony with one another; be sympathetic, love as brothers, be compassionate and humble.* 1 Peter 3:8

Article III: I believe in one, holy, catholic and apostolic Church. I confess one baptism for the forgiveness of sins, and I look forward to the resurrection of the dead and the life of the world to come. Amen.

Take-away: The church (also referred to in the Bible as "a people of God" or the "body of Christ") is to reflect the unity and oneness of the Trinity.

Truth: The people of God are a holy priesthood (1 Peter 2:9-10).

We serve the Triune God. What does this understanding mean for the Church?

I believe in **one,** holy, **catholic and apostolic Church.**

In 2010, the Lausanne Movement Theology Working Group of the Lausanne III Congress – Cape Town 2010, published a statement regarding their mission:

Mission: *The whole church taking the whole gospel to the whole world.*[12]

The "whole church" reinforces God's desire that there be no division within the body.

Read Genesis 3 in your Bible to discover what caused separation and division between God and humans, humans within themselves, humans with each other, and humans with the rest of God's creation. Write a summary of the events:

At "The Fall" all relationships were broken. Through the sacrifice of Jesus Christ, God has invited us back into right relationship with him, and right relationship with each other.

Truth: Through the gospel, we have been reconciled to God and to each other.

LESSON SIX: THE CHURCH AS A PEOPLE OF GOD

What does the scripture say about God's desire for unity and oneness?

Read and summarize Jesus' prayer to his Father in John 17:20-23:

What does Galatians 3:26-29 reveal about our relationship with God, and our relationship with each other?

How do we see this hope and promise at work in the encouragement provided to the Jews and Gentiles in Ephesians 2:11-22?
Read Ephesians 2:11-22:

> *^{11} Therefore, remember that formerly you who are Gentiles by birth and called themselves "the circumcision" (that done in the body by the hands of men)—^{12} remember that at that time you were separate from Christ, excluded from citizenship in Israel and foreigners to the covenants of the promise, without hope and without God in the world. ^{13} But now in Christ Jesus you who once were far away have been brought near through the blood of Christ. ^{14} For he himself is our peace, who has made the two one and has destroyed the barrier, the dividing wall of hostility, ^{15} by **abolishing in his flesh the law with its commandments and regulations. His purpose was to create in himself one new man out of the two, thus making peace** ^{16} and in this one body to reconcile both of them to God through the cross, by which he put to death their hostility. ^{17} He came and preached peace to you who were far away and peace to those who were near. ^{18} For through him we both have access to the Father by one Spirit. ^{19} Consequently, you are no longer foreigners and aliens, but fellow citizens with God's people and members of God's household ^{20} built on the foundation of the apostles and prophets, with Christ Jesus himself as the chief cornerstone. ^{21} In him the whole building is joined together and rises to be become a holy temple in the Lord. ^{22} And in him you too are being built together to become a dwelling in which God lives by his Spirit.*

Knowledge Checkpoint:

A. Read through this passage again, and circle every time you see the word "one" in the passage.

B. Read through this passage again, and underline every time you see the word "peace."

C. Read through this passage once more, and put a box around the phrases "in Christ Jesus," "in him," "through him," "through the blood of Christ."

As Gentiles (according to Ephesians 2:11-13), how does the scripture describe our lives before we entered into a relationship with Christ?

According to Ephesians 2:13-18, what has Christ made possible for us?

According to Ephesians 2:15, what was Jesus' purpose? How does this offer us hope?

Because of this work of Christ, what kind of people are we called to be in this world? Reference Ephesians 2:19-20.

In verses 19-22, we see the metaphor of a house being used to describe "God's people" or "God's household." What mental picture does this image provide for us? What might it physically look like for us to live as "a holy temple in the Lord"? Write specific examples.

LESSON SIX: THE CHURCH AS A PEOPLE OF GOD

Read 2 Corinthians 5:14-21. Write a paragraph summary of what is being communicated in this passage:

What hope do we have to live as a reconciled people—people who are reconciled to God, and people who are reconciled with each other?

Read Colossians 1:19-23. According to these passages, what hope do we have to live as a reconciled people?

Truth: The people of God are called to live holy lives.

> *I believe in* **one,** *holy*, **catholic and apostolic Church:**

Write down the scripture Leviticus 22:31-33:

Write down the scripture Hebrews 12:14:

Read 1 Peter 1:15-25 in your Bible. Summarize what you learned from these verses:

LESSON SIX: THE CHURCH AS A PEOPLE OF GOD

Write down the scripture 1 Peter 1:15-16:

According to these scriptures, how does holiness unite the people of God? Hint: You can also reference 1 Corinthians 1:2.

Summary: We are made holy by Christ, and we have a choice and responsibility to live holy lives. Through the grace of God and the power of the Holy Spirit, holiness reveals that faith is at work in us.

> *I believe in* **one**, *holy*, **catholic** *and* **apostolic Church:**

According to the Lausanne Movement "The Whole Church taking the Whole Gospel to the Whole World (Condensed) report:

> *The word "catholic" in the creed speaks of the universal church—which is another meaning of "the whole church." The church of God is* **universal in its membership,** *for it is open to*

people from any and every nation. It is **universal in its extent,** *for it knows no geographical boundary. It is* **universal in time and eternity,** *for it includes all God's people drawn from all generation of human history. And it is* **universal in the eyes of God,** *for the Lord knows those who are his.*[13]

Knowledge Checkpoint: What are the four ways that the church is universal?

1.

2.

3.

4.

What does the Word of God say about this reality?
Read Galatians 3:26-28:

> [26] *You are all sons of God through faith in Christ Jesus.* [27] *for all of you who were baptized into Christ have clothed yourselves with Christ.* [28] *There is neither Jew nor Greek, slave nor free, male nor female, for you are all one in Christ Jesus.*

What do we learn about Christ's view of the people who come into his family in this passage?

Read Revelation 5:9-10:

> [9] *And they sang a new song:*
> *"You are worthy to take the scroll*
> *and to open its seals,*
> *because you were slain,*
> *and with your blood you purchased men for God*
> *from every tribe and language and*
> *people and nation.*
> [10] *You have made them to be kingdom and priests to serve our God,*
> *and they will reign on the earth."*

LESSON SIX: THE CHURCH AS A PEOPLE OF GOD

This scripture is a vision of the worship Christ will receive in Heaven. According to this text, what has the sacrificial blood of Christ done for people?

What types of people groups are mentioned in this passage?

In Revelation Chapter 7, the writer John shares his vision and mentions the tribes of Israel, God's chosen people, that will be sealed for salvation. After he mentioned those tribes, he wrote:

> *⁹ After this I looked and there before me was a great multitude that no one could count from every **nation, tribe, people and language, standing before the throne and in front of the Lamb**. They were wearing white robes and were holding palm branches in their hands. ¹⁰ And they cried out in a loud voice:*
> *"Salvation belongs to our God,*
> *Who sits on the throne,*
> *And to the Lamb."*

What types of people groups are mentioned in this passage?

What hope does this scripture offer for us?

Mission: The whole church taking the whole gospel to the **whole world**.[14]

These scriptures confirm God's desire to reveal himself to the whole world, even though the whole world might not accept him.

Read John 3:16-21 in your Bible. What do you learn about God's desires in these passages?

> *I believe in* **one,** *holy*, **catholic and apostolic Church:**

According to the Lausanne Movement "The Whole Church taking the Whole Gospel to the Whole World (Condensed) report:

> The apostolic nature of the church has three biblical meanings:
>
> a) Historical: that the church is founded on the historic apostles of Jesus Christ. Their authorized witness to Christ, in word, deed and in the writings of the New Testament, along with their acceptance of the authority of the Old Testament scriptures, constitute the primary authoritative and final source of our ecclesiology;
> b) Doctrinal: that we are called to be faithful to the teaching of the apostles, by our submission to the authority of Scripture; and
> c) Missional: that we are to carry forward the mission of the apostles in bearing witness to God's saving work in Christ.

> The church exists as the community of faith in fellowship with the apostles; and we are called to live as those who are "sent" in mission as the apostles were sent by the risen Christ.
>
> To speak of the church as "apostolic" is another way of saying that the church is missional by definition. It cannot be otherwise and be church. Mission is not something we add to the identity and role of the church, but is intrinsic to it.[15]

In short, the words "apostolic" and "mission" both refer to "sending." The English language takes the noun for the person who is sent (apostle) from the Greek language, and the noun for the act of sending (mission) from Latin, so the connection and emphasis on "sending" is not always clear in the English language. As Christians, we must be conscious of how we are sending disciples into the world to proclaim the grace and good news of Christ Jesus wherever they go.

Mission: The whole church taking the whole gospel to the whole world.[16]

What is this mission that Christ has called us to?

There are several scriptures that present the Great Commission to share the gospel (or "good news" of Jesus) by making disciples.[17] The most familiar passage is Matthew 28:18-20:

> *[18] Jesus came to them and said, "All authority in heaven and on earth has been given to me. [19] Therefore go and make disciples of all nations, baptizing them in the name of the Father and of the Son and of the Holy Spirit, [20] and teaching them to obey everything I have commanded you. And surely I am with you always, to the very end of the age."*

This commission is what motivated me to write the book, *Mentor for Life: Finding Purpose through Intentional Discipleship*. In it, I approach mentoring from the perspective of intentional discipleship. The first chapter invites people to "Join the Mission" of God. That mission is simply to prioritize the "Great Commandment" to love and the "Great Commission" to make disciples.

When we approach mentoring as intentional discipleship, we are living into the apostolic nature of the church. Mentoring in this way is missional:

It is an intentional approach to discipleship that is progressive first, by inspiring mentees [those we mentor] to *know and love God*; second, by helping mentees understand *who they are in Christ* [this is a question about identity]; and finally, by encouraging mentees to *love their neighbors* as they love themselves.[18] This progressive mentoring framework places the whole gospel at center stage and reminds us that the church's most crucial mission is making disciples, which is a serious responsibility for *every* believer.[19]

Mentoring as intentional discipleship enhances the missional focus of the universal church by raising up mission-minded leaders:

Nurturing Christian leaders of character begins with mentoring. We often miss opportunities to train up leaders in the church because of the misconception that some are leaders—mostly due to their titles, hierarchy, gender, or ordination—and others are not.

This misconception causes many Christians to settle for a complacent life of waiting for someone to tell them what to do, and if no one engages them, they don't act. Mentoring addresses this leadership challenge by making all believers aware of their responsibilities to live on purpose and commit to God's mission. This paradigm shift is a blessing for the church and a means of God's grace to the world. A God-focused and God-purposed mentoring relationship stretches and changes the way we view mentoring *and* leadership alike. So not only is mentoring a means of intentional discipleship, it is a leadership factory that prepares people of all backgrounds, life stages, and experiences to lead well.[20]

This is your missional challenge:

Mentoring as intentional discipleship allows us to influence others so they forsake the indulgences of this life in exchange for a spirit-filled, life-giving, other-focused existence.
This is your mission. I invite you to take action! We make this mentoring commitment with the declaration that we are God's church, committed to living on purpose and to advancing God's kingdom. Together, we can embody the biblical vision of the Lausanne Movement: The whole church taking the whole gospel to the whole world…" Together, we can change the culture in the church and equip all God's people for service.[21] Will you join this mission?[22]

Summary: Understanding the apostolic nature of the church, embracing the missional focus of the church, and committing to mentoring as intentional discipleship, prepares the whole church to take the whole gospel to the whole world.

What is your response to this challenge?

I confess one baptism for the forgiveness of sins, and I look forward to the resurrection of the dead and the life of the world to come. Amen.

LESSON SIX: THE CHURCH AS A PEOPLE OF GOD

> One baptism for the remission of sins:

Write down the definition of baptism –

What does the Word of God say about baptism?

Write down the scripture Ephesians 4:4-6:

What is the significance of this scripture in the life of a believer (anyone who believes that Jesus is God or professes faith in Jesus Christ)?

A relative of Jesus and prophet, John the Baptist, spoke of baptism in this way in Matthew 3:11:[23]

> "I baptize you with water for repentance. But after me will come one [Jesus] who is more powerful than I, whose sandals I am not fit to carry. He will baptize you with the Holy Spirit and with fire."

John the Baptist baptized Jesus in Matthew 3:13-17. According to verse 15, what was the purpose of Jesus' own baptism?

Jesus explained the baptism that he offers in a conversation with Nicodemus in John 3:1-15. Read and then summarize this passage below:

In this passage, Jesus speaks of offering a supernatural birth (John 1:12-13). This birth happens through the work of the Holy Spirit, by the act of repentance.
Write down the definition of repentance:

This new birth gives us the eternal life that Jesus mentions. The Old Testament gives a proper context of what Nicodemus would have understood from his conversation with Jesus. Read what God spoke in Ezekiel 36:25-27:

LESSON SIX: THE CHURCH AS A PEOPLE OF GOD

> *^{25} I will sprinkle clean water on you, and you will be clean; I will cleanse you from all your impurities and from all your idols. ^{26} I will give you a new heart and put a new spirit in you; I will remove from you your heart of stone and give you a heart of flesh. ^{27} And I will put my Spirit in you and move you to follow my decrees and be careful to keep my laws.*

Given these scriptures, what hope does baptism for the remission of sins offer us?

The resurrection of the dead

At this point, we know that Christ died for our sins on the cross. However, that is not the end of the story. After three days, Christ rose from the dead. Christ himself has been resurrected!

The truth of his resurrection, which Jesus promised would come, is confirmed in Matthew 28:5-6, Mark 16:6-7, and Luke 24:5-8. The Gospel of John, Chapters 20 and 21, records detailed accounts of Jesus' earthly encounters with his disciples after his resurrection.

Read 1 Corinthians Chapter 15, and write a summary of what you have learned about the resurrection:

Christ's resurrection is a central truth to the Christian faith. Read what Paul, a follower of Christ, says about the significance of the resurrection in 1 Corinthians 15:12-19:

> *^{12} But if it is preached that Christ has been raised from the dead, how can some of you say that there is no resurrection of the dead? ^{13} If there is no resurrection of the death, then not even Christ has been raised. ^{14} And if Christ has not been raised, our preaching is useless and so is your faith. ^{15} **More than that, we are then found to be false witnesses about God, for we have testified about God** that he raised Christ from the dead. But he did not raise him if in fact the dead are not raised. ^{16} For if the dead are not raised, then Christ has not been raised either. ^{17} And if Christ has not been raised, your faith if futile; you are still in your sins. ^{18} **Then those also who have fallen asleep in Christ are lost.** ^{19} If only for this life we have hope in Christ, we are to be pitied more than all men.*

What hope and assurance does the resurrection of Christ offer us?

Summary: There is great debate among Christian scholars about when the resurrection of the dead will take place or when Jesus will return to take us to live with him forever, but Christians collectively agree that the resurrection of the dead and eternal life with Jesus will happen for every believer. We have this hope and promise because of Jesus' own resurrection.

Eternal life in the world to come

We have already surveyed Scriptures from the book of Revelation that provide a glimpse into the worship and fellowship we will experience in eternity with the Lord. He will be our God, and we will be his united people. We will praise him forever. Amen.

In 1 Corinthians 15:20-26, the Apostle Paul continues his instruction concerning the resurrection of Jesus Christ and what that means for the world to come:

> [20] *But Christ has indeed been raised from the dead, the firstfruits of those who have fallen asleep.* [21] *For since death came through a man, the resurrection of the dead comes also through a man.* [22] *For as in Adam all die, so in Christ all will be made alive.* [23] *But each in his own turn: Christ, the firstfruits; then, when he comes, those who belong to him.* [24] *Then the end will come, when he hands over the kingdom to God the Father after he has destroyed all dominion, authority and power.* [25] *For he must reign until he has put all his enemies under his feet.* [26] **The last enemy to be destroyed is death.**

What distinctions does this passage put between the world that we currently live in, and the new world that is to come?

What hope does this passage offer for us?

Genesis Chapters 1 and 2 describe the world as God originally intended. It was a "very good," indeed perfect, world until sin entered the picture with the disobedience of Adam (also known as "The Fall") as recorded in Genesis Chapter 3. Since Adam (the first man) served as our human representative before God, his sin (also known as the "original sin") negatively impacted all God's creation. The entire Bible is God's redemption story revealing all the ways God pursues his human creation, and seeks to draw us back into right relationship with himself.

LESSON SIX: THE CHURCH AS A PEOPLE OF GOD

His loving efforts for reconciliation are most visible in the sacrifice of his Son, Jesus. Because of this sacrifice, we—those of us who trust in Jesus for our salvation—are able to enter into right relationship with God, ourselves, each other, and the rest of creation.

The assurance of our salvation also gives us great hope for the eternal future we will spend in God's presence, where we will worship God forever; dwell in harmony together; and where our common enemy, Satan, will have no dominion. This new world will have no end.

John, a disciple of Jesus, gives us a vision of this new world. Read and write a summary of what we have to look forward to according to Revelation Chapters 21-22:

How has this study shaped your knowledge and love of the Triune God? Write specifically about your understanding of the relationship between God, the Father; God, the Son; and God, the Holy Spirit.

What hope has this study of the Nicene Creed offered you?

How has this study impacted the way you view yourself and your purpose in the world?

How will this study impact the way you view and interact with others? Write specifically about how this study of the Nicene Creed will impact how you engage those who are Christians, and those who are not.

Natasha's Prayer: *Lord, I pray that you will use the truth of these words to continue to speak to the heart of the person who has completed this study. I pray that you will become their dear and close friend, as they acknowledge the hope that you offer in their <u>salvation</u>. Please clarify their purpose and calling in this world, in your Son, Jesus' name. Amen.*

LIST OF DEFINITIONS

Almighty	having absolute power over all[24]
Archetype	the original or model of which all things of the same type are representations or copies; prototype[25]
baptism	The practice of sprinkling with, pouring on or immersing in water as an act of Christian initiation and obedience to Christ's own command[26]
begotten	to procreate as the father; to bring into being[27]
blasphemy	insulting, cursing, lacking reverence for God; claiming deity[28]
condemnation	judicial pronouncement upon a guilty person, *punishment, penalty*. "There is no death-sentence for those who are in Christ Jesus."[29]
conviction	1. To scrutinize or examine carefully, 2. To bring a person to the point of recognizing wrongdoing, 3. To express strong disapproval of someone's action, or 4. To penalize for wrongdoing, punish, discipline[30]
covenant	refers to the act of God in freely establishing a mutually binding relationship with humankind… [Throughout the Bible,] God made covenants with Noah, Abraham, Moses and David. But above all, God has fulfilled these covenants and has inaugurated the New Covenant in Christ, which is for all people who trust in him (Hebrews 9:15, 27-28).[31]
deity	The rank or essential nature of god; one exalted or revered as supremely good or powerful[32]
disciple	The Greek term disciple (*mathetes*) means learner, student, or apprentice…A disciple as a student or apprentice is attached to a rabbi or teacher…This apprenticeship model of rabbi to student is an ongoing status throughout life…At the heart of all disciples is the desire to be like their teacher in character and action, in all things (Colossians 3:17). In order for this to occur, disciples must arrange their lives for this type of training. This arrangement is what we call discipleship.[33]
divine	of, relating to, or proceeding directly from God; supremely good[34]
ecclesiology	The area of theological study concerned with understanding the church (derived from the Greek word ἐκκλησία, "church"). Ecclesiology seeks to set forth the nature and function of the church. It also investigates issues such as the mission, ministry and structure of the church, as well as its role in the overall plan of God.[35]

essence	(essentia) Deriving from the Latin verb *esse*, literally "to be," essence is the fundamental nature of something apart from which the thing would not be what it is. Essence, then, is the core of what makes something what it is without being something else.[36]
eternal	having infinity duration, of or relating to eternity, characterized by abiding fellowship with God[37] Eternal life also refers not just to the *length* of life, but also to *quality* of life and our experience of wholeness and union with God. In eternal life, we experience now something of the splendor, joy, and peace that are characteristic of the life of God… In the present stage of eternal life, our trust in Christ grows so that our character is progressively transformed into Christlikeness.[38]
glory	splendor; honor; renown; fullness of perfection[39]
grace	The words in the original languages of the Bible translated as grace mean undeserved favor, kindness, and benevolence…Theologians distinguish common grace from special grace…While God's special grace pertains to salvation, common grace signifies the undeserved favor he extends universally to all humans—believers and unbelievers alike—in the form of earthly and material blessings.[40]
holy	exalted or worthy of complete devotion as one perfect in goodness and righteousness[41]
idol	a representation or symbol of an object of worship; a false god[42]
incarnation	the embodiment of a deity or spirit in some earthly form; the union of divinity with humanity in Jesus Christ[43]
metaphor	a figure of speech in which a word or phrase literally denoting one kind of object or idea is used in place of another to suggest a likeness or analogy between them[44]
monotheism	The belief in one God (*mono-theos*) as opposed to belief in many gods (*polytheism*).[45]
perish	to become destroyed or ruined[46]
prophet	inspired messenger who declares the will of God[47]
reconciliation	A change in relationship or attitude from enmity to peace…Reconciliation is a central doctrine of Christianity. Specifically, in Christ God reconciled the sinful, hostile world to himself by Christ's taking upon himself the cost of our hostility and enmity, thereby setting the world free to restored union with God (2 Cor. 5:19).[48]
redemption	the process by which sinful humans are "bought back" from the bondage of sin into relationship with God through grace by the "payment" of Jesus' death.[49]
remission	to release from the guilt or penalty of; to restore or consign to a former status or condition[50]

LIST OF DEFINITIONS

repentance Repentance carries two central ideas from the Old and New Testaments: (1) turning back to God, and (2) doing so as a willful decision…Repentance isn't a one-time action. Instead, it's an ongoing disposition of our will to always rely on God, to believe that what he says is true and trustworthy, and to live in his freedom (Galatians 5:1). Repentance is the doorway to life in God, and it's something we must do. While God offers forgiveness to us when we repent, he will not ask repentance for us. It's our requirement for entering and living in his kingdom.[51]

resurrection the central, defining doctrine and claim of the Christian faith is the resurrection of Jesus Christ, whom God brought forth from the dead. The resurrection of the dead refers to the promise based on the bodily resurrection of Jesus, that all believers will one day join Christ in the resurrection. Believers will be transformed, that is, renewed both morally and physically with "spiritual" bodies adapted for eternal life with God.[52]

salvation A broad term referring to God's activity on behalf of creation and especially humans in bringing all things to God's intended goal. More specifically, salvation entails God's deliverance of humans from the power and effects of sin and the Fall through the work of Jesus Christ so that creation in general and humans in particular can enjoy the fullness of life intended for what God has made.[53]

Trinity The Christian understanding of God as triune. Trinity means that the one divine nature is a unity of three persons and that God is revealed as three distinct persons: Father, Son and Holy Spirit.[54]

triune three in one[55]

24. A Biblical Presentation of the Trinity

Introduction	The word "Trinity" is never used, nor is the doctrine of Trinitarianism ever explicitly taught in the Scriptures, but Trinitarianism is the best explication of the biblical evidence. The theological exposition of the doctrine arose from clear, but not comprehensive, scriptural teaching. It is a crucial doctrine for Christianity because it focuses on who God is, and particularly on the deity of Jesus Christ. Because Trinitarianism is not taught explicitly in the Scriptures, the study of the doctrine is an exercise in putting together biblical themes and data through a systematic theological study and through looking at the historical development of the present orthodox view of what the biblical presentation of the Trinity is.
Essential Elements of the Trinity	1. God is One. 2. Each of the persons within the Godhead is Deity. 3. The oneness of God and the threeness of God are not contradictory. 4. The Trinity (Father, Son, and Holy Spirit) is eternal. 5. Each of the persons of God is of the same essence and is not inferior or superior to the others in essence. 6. The Trinity is a mystery which we will never be able to understand fully.

Biblical Teaching	Old Testament	New Testament
God is One	Hear, O Israel: The LORD our God, the LORD is one (Deut 6:4; cf. 20:2-3; 3:13-15).	Now to the King eternal, immortal, invisible, the only God, be honor and glory for ever and ever. Amen (1 Tim. 1:17; cf. 1 Cor. 8:4-6; 1 Tim. 2:5-6; James 2:19).
Three Distinct Persons as Deity	The Father: He said to me, "You are my Son; today I have become your Father" (Ps. 2:7).	. . . who have been chosen according to the foreknowledge of God the Father . . . (1 Peter 1:2; cf. John 1:17; 1 Cor. 8:6; Phil. 2:11).
	The Son: He said to me, "You are my Son; today I have become your Father" (Ps. 2:7; cf. Heb. 1:1-13; Ps. 68:18; Isa. 6:1-3; 9:6).	As soon as Jesus was baptized, he went up out of the water. At that moment heaven was opened, and he saw the Spirit of God descending like a dove and lighting on him. And a voice from heaven said, "This is my Son, whom I love; with him I am well pleased" (Matt. 3:16-17).
	The Holy Spirit: In the beginning God created the heavens and the earth . . . and the Spirit of God was hovering over the waters (Gen. 1:1-2; cf. Exod. 31:3; Judg. 15:14; Isa. 11:2).	Then Peter said, "Ananias, how is it that Satan has so filled your heart that you have lied to the Holy Spirit . . . ? You have not lied to men but to God" (Acts 5:3-4; cf. 2 Cor. 3:17).

22. Ancient Diagram of the Holy Trinity

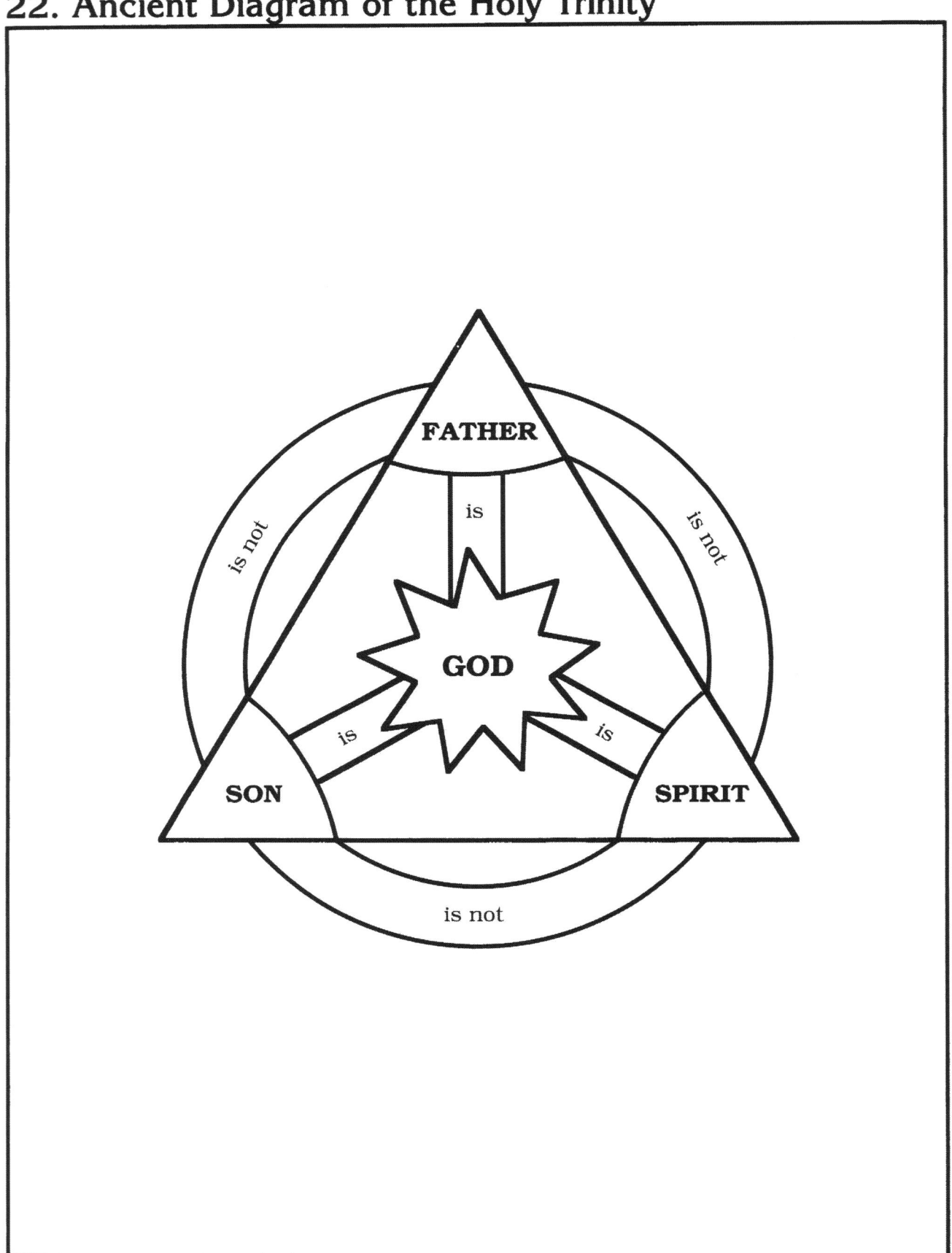

68

24. A Biblical Presentation of the Trinity (continued)

Plurality of Persons in the Godhead	The use of plural pronouns points to, or at least suggests, the plurality of persons within the Godhead in the Old Testament. "Then God said, 'Let us make man in our image, in our likeness. . . .'"	The use of the singular word "name" when referring to God the Father, Son, and Holy Spirit indicates a unity within the threeness of God. "Therefore go and make disciples of all nations, baptizing them in the name of the Father and of the Son and of the Holy Spirit" (Matt. 28:19).

	Attribute	Father	Son	Holy Spirit
Persons of the Same Essence: Attributes Applied to Each Person	Eternality	Ps. 90:2	John 1:2; Rev. 1:8, 17	Heb. 9:14
	Power	1 Peter 1:5	2 Cor. 12:9	Rom. 15:19
	Omniscience	Jer. 17:10	Rev. 2:23	1 Cor. 2:11
	Omnipresence	Jer. 23:24	Matt. 18:20	Ps. 139:7
	Holiness	Rev. 15:4	Acts 3:14	Acts 1:8
	Truth	John 7:28	Rev. 3:7	1 John 5:6
	Benevolence	Rom. 2:4	Eph. 5:25	Neh. 9:20
Equality with Different Roles: Activities Involving All Three Persons	Creation of the World	Ps. 102:25	Col. 1:16	Gen. 1:2; Job 26:13
	Creation of Man	Gen. 2:7	Col. 1:16	Job 33:4
	Baptism of Christ	Matt. 3:17	Matt. 3:16	Matt. 3:16
	Death of Christ	Heb. 9:14	Heb. 9:14	Heb. 9:14

ENDNOTES

1. This western version of the Nicene Creed includes the language "and the Son;" however, the version of the creed approved at the council in 381 did not include this language. This language was added much later by Roman Catholics, and it has never been accepted by the Eastern Orthodox churches. Historical note: The establishment of Charlemagne empire in 800 divided the Christian church into the East and West. Western churches either gravitated around Rome or broke away from her at the Reformation. Eastern churches originally depended on the Eastern Empire of Constantinople.
2. The Editors of Encyclopedia Britannica, "Nicene Creed," Encyclopedia Britannica, Inc., https://www.britannica.com/topic/Nicene-Creed (accessed September 21, 2017).
3. A.W. Tozer, The Knowledge of the Holy (New York: HarperCollins, 1961), 1.
4. For a detailed treatment of the events leading to the Nicene Creed, see chapters 2-4 of the following book: Donald M. Fairbairn Jr., The Story of Creeds and Confessions (Grand Rapids, MI: Baker Academic).
5. The word "ecumenical" derived from the Greek word oikoumenē, "signifying the entire inhabited world. In early biblical usage, the word implies the global scope of the Christian mission. However, over time and with usage, the term has developed three other meanings. First, the term is frequently used to denote the common confessions, such as the Nicene creed, that unite all branches of Christianity…Second, the term ecumenical is also used to refer to interreligious dialog between Christian and non-Christian religious groups as well as to the need for greater cooperation among other Christian groups…Finally, the term has come full circle to refer to the emergence of global Christianity of which we (despite our various denominations) are all participants."
Timothy C. Tennent, Theology in the context of World Christianity (Grand Rapids, MI: Zondervan, 2007), 185.
6. Leclercq, H. (1911). The First Council of Nicaea. In The Catholic Encyclopedia. New York: Robert Appleton Company. Retrieved September 4, 2017 from New Advent: http://www.newadvent.org/cathen/11044a.htm
7. When we say, "Catholic Church," today we are not referring to the Roman Catholic Church, but rather the entire church or people of God at all times, and throughout all places.
Roger E. Olson, The Story of Christian Theology: Twenty Centuries of Tradition & Reform (Downer Grove, IL: IVP Academic, 1999), 278.
8. Davidson, 98.
9. Davidson, 98.
10. Reference Psalm 82:6.
11. This western version of the Nicene Creed includes the language "and the Son;" however, the version of the creed approved at the council in 381 did not include this language. This language was added much later and has never been accepted by the Eastern Church.

    On a separate note: "acknowledgement of the deity of the Holy Spirit must not be confused with a full affirmation of the Trinity. The Trinity was officially reaffirmed in the fifth ecumenical council in Constantinople in 553."
Timothy C. Tennent, Theology in the context of World Christianity (Grand Rapids, MI: Zondervan, 2007), 171.

12. Theology Working Group, "The Whole Church taking the Whole Gospel to the Whole World," Lausanne Movement, https://www.lausanne.org/content/twg-three-wholes (accessed June 10, 2010).
13. Theology Working Group, The Whole Church taking the Whole Gospel to the Whole World (Condensed), Lausanne Movement, https://www.lausanne.org/content/twg-three-wholes-condensed (accessed February 15, 2017).
14. Theology Working Group, "The Whole Church taking the Whole Gospel to the Whole World," Lausanne Movement, https://www.lausanne.org/content/twg-three-wholes (accessed June 10, 2010).
15. Theology Working Group, The Whole Church taking the Whole Gospel to the Whole World (Condensed), Lausanne Movement, https://www.lausanne.org/content/twg-three-wholes-condensed

(accessed February 15, 2017).

16 Theology Working Group, "The Whole Church taking the Whole Gospel to the Whole World," Lausanne Movement, https://www.lausanne.org/content/twg-three-wholes (accessed June 10, 2010).

17 In addition to Matthew 28:18-20, read Mark 16:15, Luke 24:47-49, and John 20:21.

18 Matthew 22:37-39; Mark 12:30-31; Luke 10:27; Deuteronomy 6:5; and Leviticus 19:18.

19 Natasha Sistrunk Robinson, Mentor for Life: Finding Purpose through Intentional Discipleship (Grand Rapids, MI: Zondervan, 2016), 35.

20 Natasha Sistrunk Robinson, Mentor for Life: Finding Purpose through Intentional Discipleship (Grand Rapids, MI: Zondervan, 2016), 36.

21 Reference Ephesians 2:9-10 and Ephesians 4:11-16.

22 Natasha Sistrunk Robinson, Mentor for Life: Finding Purpose through Intentional Discipleship (Grand Rapids, MI: Zondervan, 2016), 38.

23 Also reference Mark 1:8 and Luke 3:16.

24 Merriam-Wester, "Dictionary search Almighty," Merriam-Webster, Incorporated, https://www.merriam-webster.com/dictionary/almighty (accessed September 18, 2017).

25 Merriam-Wester, "Dictionary search Archetype," Merriam-Webster, Incorporated, https://www.merriam-webster.com/dictionary/archetype (accessed September 18, 2017).

26 Stanley J. Grenz, David Guretzki & Cherith Fee Nordling, Pocket Dictionary of Theological Terms (Downers Grove, IL: InterVarsity Press, 1999), 18.

27 Thomas Nelson Publishers, The Three-In-One Bible Reference Companion (Nashville, TN: Thomas Nelson Publishers, 1982), 73.

28 Thomas Nelson Publishers, The Three-In-One Bible Reference Companion (Nashville, TN: Thomas Nelson Publishers, 1982), 88.

29 Bauer, Walter, William F. Arndt, F. Wilbur Gingrich, and Frederick W. Danker. A Greek-English Lexicon of the New Testament and Other Early Christian Literature, 3rd ed. Chicago: University of Chicago Press, 2000.

30 Bauer, Walter, William F. Arndt, F. Wilbur Gingrich, and Frederick W. Danker. A Greek-English Lexicon of the New Testament and Other Early Christian Literature, 3rd ed. Chicago: University of Chicago Press, 2000.

31 Stanley J. Grenz, David Guretzki & Cherith Fee Nordling, Pocket Dictionary of Theological Terms (Downers Grove, IL: InterVarsity Press, 1999), 32.

32 Merriam-Wester, "Dictionary search Deity," Merriam-Webster, Incorporated, https://www.merriam-webster.com/dictionary/deity (accessed September 19, 2017).

33 Bruce Demarest and Keith J. Matthews, eds., Dictionary of Everyday Theology and Culture (Colorado Springs, CO: NavPress, 2010), 115-116.

34 Merriam-Wester, "Dictionary search Divine," Merriam-Webster, Incorporated, https://www.merriam-webster.com/dictionary/divine (accessed September 19, 2017).

35 Stanley J. Grenz, David Guretzki & Cherith Fee Nordling, Pocket Dictionary of Theological Terms (Downers Grove, IL: InterVarsity Press, 1999), 42.

36 Stanley J. Grenz, David Guretzki & Cherith Fee Nordling, Pocket Dictionary of Theological Terms (Downers Grove, IL: InterVarsity Press, 1999), 46.

37 Merriam-Wester, "Dictionary search Eternal," Merriam-Webster, Incorporated, https://www.merriam-webster.com/dictionary/eternal (accessed September 19, 2017).

38 Bruce Demarest and Keith J. Matthews, eds., Dictionary of Everyday Theology and Culture (Colorado Springs, CO: NavPress, 2010), 131.

39 Thomas Nelson Publishers, The Three-In-One Bible Reference Companion (Nashville, TN: Thomas Nelson Publishers, 1982), 289.

40 Bruce Demarest and Keith J. Matthews, eds., Dictionary of Everyday Theology and Culture (Colorado Springs, CO: NavPress, 2010), 200.

41 Merriam-Wester, "Dictionary search Holy," Merriam-Webster, Incorporated, https://www.merriam-webster.com/dictionary/holy (accessed September 19, 2017).

42 Merriam-Wester, "Dictionary search Idol," Merriam-Webster, Incorporated, https://www.merriam-webster.com/dictionary/idol (accessed September 19, 2017).

43 Merriam-Wester, "Dictionary search Incarnation," Merriam-Webster, Incorporated, https://www.merriam-

webster.com/dictionary/incarnation (accessed September 19, 2017).

44 Merriam-Wester, "Dictionary search Metaphor," Merriam-Webster, Incorporated, https://www.merriam-webster.com/dictionary/metaphor (accessed September 18, 2017).

45 Stanley J. Grenz, David Guretzki & Cherith Fee Nordling, Pocket Dictionary of Theological Terms (Downers Grove, IL: InterVarsity Press, 1999), 81.

46 Thomas Nelson Publishers, The Three-In-One Bible Reference Companion (Nashville, TN: Thomas Nelson Publishers, 1982), 520.

47 Thomas Nelson Publishers, The Three-In-One Bible Reference Companion (Nashville, TN: Thomas Nelson Publishers, 1982), 554.

48 Stanley J. Grenz, David Guretzki & Cherith Fee Nordling, Pocket Dictionary of Theological Terms (Downers Grove, IL: InterVarsity Press, 1999), 100.

49 Stanley J. Grenz, David Guretzki & Cherith Fee Nordling, Pocket Dictionary of Theological Terms (Downers Grove, IL: InterVarsity Press, 1999), 100.

50 Merriam-Wester, "Dictionary search Remit," Merriam-Webster, Incorporated, https://www.merriam-webster.com/dictionary/remit (accessed September 19, 2017).

51 Bruce Demarest and Keith J. Matthews, eds., Dictionary of Everyday Theology and Culture (Colorado Springs, CO: NavPress, 2010), 331-332.

52 Stanley J. Grenz, David Guretzki & Cherith Fee Nordling, Pocket Dictionary of Theological Terms (Downers Grove, IL: InterVarsity Press, 1999), 102.

53 Stanley J. Grenz, David Guretzki & Cherith Fee Nordling, Pocket Dictionary of Theological Terms (Downers Grove, IL: InterVarsity Press, 1999), 105.

54 Stanley J. Grenz, David Guretzki & Cherith Fee Nordling, Pocket Dictionary of Theological Terms (Downers Grove, IL: InterVarsity Press, 1999), 116.

55 Merriam-Wester, "Dictionary search Triune," Merriam-Webster, Incorporated, https://www.merriam-webster.com/dictionary/triune (accessed September 18, 2017).

Pages 58–60 (Chart 22. "Ancient Diagram of the Holy Trinity" and Chart 24. "A Biblical Presentation of the Trinity" Taken from Charts of Christian Theology and Doctrine by H. Wayne House, Copyright © 1992 by H. Wayne House. Used by permission of Zondervan. www.zondervan.com.

NATASHA SISTRUNK ROBINSON

Lead on purpose. Mentor for life.

Natasha Sistrunk Robinson is an international speaker, mentoring coach, and author of *A Sojourner's Truth: Choosing Freedom and Courage in a Divided World* and *Mentor for Life: Finding Purpose through Intentional Discipleship*. She is the Visionary Founder of the 501(c)(3) nonprofit, Leadership LINKS, Inc.

• SPEAKING TOPICS •

Natasha intentionally serves as a credible witness of Christ's leadership to engage, equip, and empower people to live and lead on purpose.

Leadership • Mentoring and Intentional Discipleship •
Spiritual Formation and Spiritual Disciples • Justice and Reconciliation

BIOGRAPHY

Natasha often refers to herself as a black girl from the small town of Orangeburg, South Carolina. The community rich in black history, culture, and tradition was a critical part of her formative years before leaving home to attend the United States Naval Academy. Upon her 2002 graduation, she was commissioned as an officer in the U.S. Marine Corps where she served six years as a Financial Management Officer and earned the rank of Captain. While in the military, she began her work of racial reconciliation by leading a team in diversity outreach efforts within the Naval Academy's Office of Admissions. After her military service, she worked at the Department of Homeland Security, before attending Gordon-Conwell Theological Seminary Charlotte where she completed independent studies on racial reconciliation and biblical justice before graduating *cum laude* with a M.A. in Leadership.

Today, Natasha works in full-time ministry as a nonprofit leader, anti-human trafficking advocate, leadership and mentoring coach, freelance writer, and international speaker. When she is not working, she enjoys reading, dancing, watching movies, eating great food, and spending time with family and friends. She resides in North Carolina with her husband and daughter.

CONTACT US

Email: bookings@natashaSrobinson.com | Web: www.natashaSrobinson.com
Blog: www.asistasjourney.com
Facebook: NatashaSistrunkRobinson | Twitter: asistasjourney | Instagram: asistasjourney

NATASHA SISTRUNK ROBINSON

Lead on purpose. Mentor for life.

A Sojourner's Truth invites us on the journey of a young African American girl from South Carolina to the United States Naval Academy and then into a calling as a speaker, mentor, writer, and teacher. Intertwined with Natasha Sistrunk Robinson's story is the story of Moses, a young leader who was born into a marginalized people group, resisted injustices of Pharaoh, denied the power of Egypt, and trusted God even when he did not fully understand or know where he was going. Along the way we courageously explore the spiritual and physical tensions of truth-telling, character and leadership development, and bridge building across racial/ethnic, socioeconomic, and gender lines. You are invited to bring along your story as well - to discover your own identity, explore your truth-revealing moments, to live unafraid, and to gain a deeper sense of purpose.

Order today: https://www.ivpress.com/a-sojourner-s-truth

Available everywhere books are sold on October 9, 2018.

Use #ASojournersTruth to join the conversation!

 # NATASHA SISTRUNK ROBINSON

Lead on purpose. Mentor for life.

Mentor for Life released to great endorsements from prominent leaders in the Christian faith, and raving Amazon book reviews.

AVAILABLE NOW EVERYWHERE BOOKS ARE SOLD:

In *Mentor for Life*, Natasha Sistrunk Robinson lays a solid foundation for mentoring as intentional discipleship, within the context of a small community. It is based on God's kingdom vision, and challenge followers of Christ to consider the cost of discipleship.

Filled with examples from Robinson's experience in the military and business world, this resource gives readers the wisdom and practical insight they need to disciple others. It proves an invaluable resource for pastors, small group leaders, seminary professors, and those who desire to take the initiate, make the commitment, and mentor others well.

WHAT ARE YOUR NEXT STEPS?

Once people understand the importance of making disciples, oftentimes they still lack confidence in getting started.

The Mentor for Life Leader's Training Manual accompanies the book, *Mentor for Life*, **to offer a tested and practical step-by-step training for individual mentors, lay leaders, or those who are interested in starting or refining a mentoring or discipleship ministry in their church.**

This leadership training tool is available now through the store on Natasha's official website or on Natasha's author page only at Amazon.com.

https://goo.gl/WpvmzF

Leadership LINKS, Inc. is a growing faith-based, charitable, and educational organization incorporated in the state of North Carolina. We are exempt from federal income tax under the Internal Revenue Code (IRC) Section 501(c)(3). Founded and led by veterans, Leadership LINKS, Inc. enriches communities through leadership, mentoring, and education.

WE EXIST to educate and equip servant leaders who are committed to suing their skills and resources for the greater good of humanity.

OUR MISSION is to offer leadership education that facilitates impactful living, character and spiritual development.

OUR CORE VALUES

Love   Inspiration   Network   Knowledge   Service

LINK UP WITH US

Find out more about the development of our educational resources and leadership programming, and learn how to get involved.

Email: leadershiplinksus@gmail.com | Web: www.leadershiplinksinc.org
Facebook: LeadershipLINKSInc | Twitter: LINKSLead | Instagram: leadershiplinks

Made in the USA
Columbia, SC
23 July 2021